THE

INTERNATIONAL EXHIBITION

OF

1862,

VIEWED IN ITS SPIRITUAL ASPECT.

A SERMON

PREACHED ON THE SUNDAY AFTER ITS OPENING,

BY

W. B. GALLOWAY, M.A.

INCUMBENT OF ST. MARK'S, REGENT'S PARK,
AND CHAPLAIN TO THE VISCOUNT HAWARDEN.

LESSONS OF THE MORNING, Num. xxiii. xxiv. Matt. ii.
EPISTLE, 1 Pet. ii. 19 - 25. GOSPEL, John x. 11—16.
PSALMS OF THE DAY, xix—xxiii.

LONDON:
RIVINGTONS, WATERLOO PLACE.
1862.

Price Sixpence.

In publishing this Sermon the Author defers to the request of a friend.

A SERMON,

&c.

PSALM xxii. 28.

" The kingdom is the Lord's, and He is the governor among
the nations."

WHOEVER is a close observer of the practical dealing of God towards His people, may have seen in it
much tenderness of consideration, much mingling
of mercy and blessing with His chastisements, a
gentle leading of His flock like a shepherd; causing
them to lie down in green pastures and by still
waters; giving rest and refreshment if the way be
long; preparing them beforehand by sweet and
holy peace; restoring their souls, and making them
to walk in the paths of righteousness. Even in
the dreariest passage they may trust His guidance;
even the gloomiest valley has a happy issue. The
pilgrimage of life is of intermingled good and evil;
but they are so disposed by infinite wisdom, that

the evil chastens and enhances the good which is bestowed; the good both mitigates the evil, and fortifies and prepares the soul to bear it; and all things work together for good. He will not over-drive His sheep one day, lest all the flock should die. He gathereth the lambs with His arm, and carrieth them in His bosom, and gently leadeth those that are with young. Or, to pass from the similitude of the shepherd to the office of kingly rule in peace and war, then, as before some arduous enterprise a wise commander will give his troops rest and encouragement, and make them know beforehand something of the prize to be attained, and the glory which shall follow, even so the Captain of our salvation, our good Shepherd, dealeth considerately and kindly with those whom He leadeth on, through many a peril and many a struggle, to assured victory and happiness. He gives occasionally some Pisgah view of the pro-mised inheritance, like Hannibal from the crest of the Alps pointing out to his soldiers the fair possessions which will reward their conquest; or He permits some brief foretaste of its fruits, some Eshcol specimen of its fair and peaceful clusters. Who that has had experience as a Christian, has not remarked, before unusual struggles and trials, some season of holy calm vouchsafed,—some blessed refreshment from the presence of the Lord, to ani-mate the soul, and strengthen it for duty and endurance unto the end? Has he not known some

sense of almost unaccountable peace and fellowship
with heaven steal over him, when God was just
about to call him to scenes which would exercise
all his faith, and task his utmost energies in the
great Christian conflict? Has he not found, on
some occasions, even in temporal things, the same
gracious and tender dealing of God with him,
affording seasonable opportunity of recruiting the
mind and body, when he knew not till afterwards
how graciously that rest was ordered to prepare
him for exertions of which he would otherwise
have been incapable? All such seasons of refreshment from the Lord are to be thankfully accepted
and enjoyed; but not to the forgetfulness that this
is not our permanent rest; not with the delusive
expectation of their continuing always. In vain,
like Peter on the holy mount, should we propose to
build there our tabernacles, or to prolong the celes-
tial visit. The stern duties of life soon call us
again; happy if we may carry along with us into
their field the refreshment and encouragement we
have received.

So is it also in the good and gracious providence
of God towards His people in their national or collective interests. The prophetic Word of God in
some places faithfully represents this, introducing a
period of trouble and suffering by a vision of the
glory that should follow, or by an anthem of praise
because of the victory that was in process of
achievement. Thus in the fifteenth chapter of the

Revelation of St. John we find a period of suffering and struggle presented in terms of a vision of those who were getting the victory, and a hearing of their song of praise. " And I saw as it were a sea of glass mingled with fire; and them that had gotten (or, more literally, them that were getting) the victory over the beast, and over his image, and over his mark, and over the number of his name, stand on the sea of glass, having the harps of God. And they sing the song of Moses the servant of God, and the song of the Lamb, saying, Great and marvellous are Thy works, Lord God Almighty; just and true are all Thy ways, Thou King of saints. Who shall not fear Thee, O Lord, and glorify Thy name? for Thou only art holy: for all nations shall come and worship before Thee; for Thy judgments were made manifest." That glorious vision of praise and thanksgiving introduces a period of great trial and strenuous exertion, and is, in fact, a brief foreshowing of the glory and the praise which should be accomplished in these trying events.

Something analogous to this we may see done on the theatre of human events. God permits before the time some short but joyous foreshadowing of the rest and peace of Christ's blessed kingdom. He permits it as a thing to be rejoiced in and received with the spirit of thankfulness, but not as giving assurance of stability or of continuance in the present. Let us not confound with solid and secure reality that which is but as a momentary anticipation of better things to come, a foretaste or a type and prophecy of blessings which must yet be waited for. Let us not, because the sea is momentarily calm, delude ourselves by trusting that it will no more be ruffled; but nevertheless let us take with thankfulness the tranquillity enjoyed, and hold it for a type and shadow of that which shall ere long be realized in the kingdom of Christ.

Such, brethren, seems to be the nature of that peaceful and happy interlude in which we now behold the arts and industry of the nations of the earth, together with the manifold produce of nature in every land, represented in a great and splendid meeting and exhibition in courteous and friendly rivalry, as beseems men and brethren whose happiness, whose riches and prosperity, and whose advancement in arts and commerce, are not a subject of envious jealousy, but of mutual joy and congratulation and of mutual benefit. Well is it that on such an occasion we should, both formally and in our hearts, express glory and thanksgiving to the Lord to whom the earth belongeth, and the fulness thereof; and should give a kindly welcome to men of every kindred, and nation, and people, and tongue; and should throw open our hearts to the lively impression of that courteous and brotherly fellowship, and seek that it may lead onward into the bonds of holier Christian love and union in the Lord; that it may be so used as to provoke one

another to love and to good works, and to show forth
in heart and life those kindly sentiments and graces of
the Christian character, by which Christ is honoured
before men, and His cause advanced in the world:
yea, that, though it be but for a season, it may
leave reminiscences which may survive through
all struggles and trials, and even if present concord should unhappily be broken may furnish
seeds of peace and reunion afterwards. For it is
thus with good and friendly acts, they leave behind
them an impression which, even if concord should
be broken, prepares the way for its re-establish-
ment. It is, therefore, much to be desired that
the impression carried back to other lands from
the present occasion should not be an envious
thought of England's wealth, but a kind remem-
brance of England's courtesy and brotherly feeling,
and a perception of the principles of Christian truth
and pure and scriptural faith which animate our
social life. Would to God the impression carried
away might be not such as one great visitor on one
occasion expressed, "What a fine city to sack!"
but rather that which Moses expresses as so desir-
able, "Surely this great nation is a wise and
understanding people!" or similar to that which
was irrepressibly conveyed to Balaam's mind, when
from the hill-top he beheld Israel abiding in his
tents according to their tribes, and exclaimed,
"How goodly are thy tents, O Jacob, and thy
tabernacles, O Israel! As the valleys are they

spread forth, as gardens by the river's side, as the trees of lign aloes which the Lord hath planted, and as cedar trees beside the waters. . . . The Lord his God is with him, and the shout of a king is among them." Yes, even thus let it be perceived and felt that Christ, the eternal Son of God, is with us and among us, the King of kings, and Lord of lords. And let the blessed name of Jesus be glorified among us in the presence of the nations by our dutiful, loyal, and orderly obedience to His Almighty Sovereignty; and let men take knowledge of us herein, of the principle on which the greatness of our country stands or falls.

Regard it as you will, brethren, it is a great occasion, and may serve in some sort as a landmark of progress. There may be some who regard it commercially only, and who congratulate themselves on an immense expansion in this respect since the year 1851. Of this it is not my province to speak particularly; but it is my duty to point out that this, taken by itself, is the least satisfactory of all grounds of glorying. Wealth does not tend to make men better. Wealth did not give stability to the kingdom of Crœsus. Wealth did not avert the fall of Tyre. On the contrary, commerce in itself is the least substantial of all the bases on which the security or greatness of a nation can be rested. We must build upon the rock, and not upon the sand; which, even if it were golden sand, affords no foundation fit to sustain the edifice when the rains descend, and the floods come, and the winds blow, and beat upon the house. Commerce and wealth are indeed valuable if they come as tokens of the Divine favour and blessing, and of a prosperity resulting from the eternal principles of justice and truth, strong in the foundations of the eternal throne; but of themselves they may mark only the dangerous elevation from which there is the likelier fall and the more tremendous crash. To those who view the present occasion in that mere commercial light, it may stand not simply as the second such world-wide fair and gathering of produce, but may claim to connect itself with a more venerable antiquity: for in this respect what is it beyond an expansion and development of the idea of those great Tyrian fairs, of the riches and magnificence of which the prophet Ezekiel [1] has given us so vivid a description? " O Tyrus, thou hast said, I am of perfect beauty. . . . Thy builders have perfected thy beauty. . . . The company of the Ashurites have made thy benches of ivory, brought out of the isles of Chittim. Fine linen with broidered work from Egypt was that which thou spreadest forth to be as thy main sheet [2]; blue and purple from the isles of Elishah was that which covered thee. Tarshish was thy merchant by reason of the multitude of all kind of riches;

---

[1] ch. xxvii.

[2] The " sail " here is meant figuratively. Literal ship sails require some very different substance and texture.

with silver, iron, tin, and lead, they traded in thy fairs. Javan, Tubal, and Meshech, they were thy merchants: they traded the persons of men and vessels of brass in thy markets. They of the house of Togarmah traded in thy fairs. . . . The men of Dedan were thy merchants; many isles were the merchandise of thine hand: they brought thee for a present horns of ivory and ebony. Syria was thy merchant by reason of the multitude of the wares of thy making: they occupied in thy fairs with emeralds, purple, and broidered work, and fine linen, and coral, and agate. Judah and the land of Israel, they were thy merchants: they traded in thy market wheat of Minnith, and Pannag, and honey, and oil, and balm. Damascus was thy merchant in the multitude of the wares of thy making, for the multitude of all riches; in the wine of Helbon, and white wool. Dan also and Javan going to and fro occupied in thy fairs; bright iron, cassia, and calamus, were in thy market. Dedan was thy merchant in precious cloths for chariots. Arabia and all the princes of Kedar, they occupied with thee. . . . . The merchants of Sheba and Raamah, they occupied in thy fairs with chief of all spices, and with precious stones, and gold. Haran, and Canneh, and Eden, the merchants of Sheba, Asshur, and Chilmad, were thy merchants. These were thy merchants in all sorts of things, in blue cloths, and broidered work, and in chests of rich apparel, bound with cords, and made of cedar, among thy merchandise." In sooth, it must have been a goodly sight to walk through one of these great Tyrian fairs, and see the representatives of these many nations in all their rich and varied costumes, and to inform the mind with knowledge of the products and arts of so many countries as were exhibited in the several courts and compartments which these occupied in her grand international bazaars; and to see on this or that occasion the ambassadors of some new country or far island of the east, which had just been brought into the extending range of commerce, walk up the midst with the air of indifference, in the consciousness that they were themselves the observed of all observers.

But the splendour of her international fairs only rendered more tremendous to Tyre, and more astounding to the nations, the news that she was broken and destroyed in the midst of the seas.

This mere commercial aspect of the occasion is therefore not the most consolatory or assuring. But there is another light in which God grant that we may be permitted rather to regard it! It is the office of faith to render all things belonging to this present perishable life subservient to the kingdom of Christ: and the riches and the manifold productions of this earth may be held and enjoyed in subordination to His glory, and in holy submission to His will; yea, may be so used and consecrated, as to furnish abounding occasions of brotherly kind-

ness and Christian charity, and to bring in a re-
venue of gratitude and praise to the Creator and
Redeemer of the world. The prophetic visions
which the Spirit of God hath furnished of the
future commonwealth and city of the saints upon
this earth present no picture of affected poverty
indolently neglecting the improvement of God's
gifts in nature and providence, no listless long-
drawn vista of bare-footed mendicants, robed in
the professional rough garment of quasi-humility.
For truly humility might be, and was, as great in
Abraham the father of the faithful, with his ex-
ceeding many flocks and herds, and treasures of
gold and silver, as in that poorest of his faithful
children, the beggar Lazarus, who at death was
carried to his congenial bosom. Riches well used
as a stewardship for God become a source of blessing; though, if trusted in, they exclude from the
kingdom of heaven. And in those glorious visions
of the future commonwealth and kingdom of the
saints which are recorded in Scripture, we find it
written, that " the nations of them that are saved
shall walk in the light of it, and the kings of the
earth shall bring their glory and honour into it;
and they shall bring the glory and honour of the
nations into it." And that the blessed Redeemer,
the King of saints, is to receive these things all
consecrated to His honour, we find proclaimed by
the voice of all heaven, " Worthy is the Lamb that
was slain to receive power, and riches, and wisdom,

and strength, and honour, and glory, and blessing."
Was it not signified even in His cradle, in the
offering then brought to Him of gold and frankin-
cense and myrrh? Yea, that all created things
are to be consecrated to Him that sitteth on the
throne, and to be held and used for His glory, is
declared in the homage of the crowned elders, saying, "Thou art worthy, O Lord, to receive glory,
and honour, and power ; *for Thou hast created all
things, and for Thy pleasure they are, and were
created.*"

In which, then, of these two aspects are we to
regard the present occasion? Is England to follow
in the wake of commercial Tyre, and be broken
like her in the midst of the seas, furnishing but a
more tremendous example of God's purpose to stain
the pride of all glory, and to bring into contempt
all the honourable of the earth? Or is she to lead
in the van of nations in bringing the riches, and
glory, and power of this world into just subser-
viency and consecration to the kingdom and glory
of Christ? Look we back, or look we forward?
Look we earthward, or look we heavenward? Amid
the perishing old fabric of the world, when the
hour of judgment is on the stroke, these are mo-
mentous questions: and they should be considered
not with a view to vain and listless speculative
opinion, but that, with all our zeal and energy, we
may strive for our part to *influence* the answer,
and to cast the scale for the kingdom and glory of

Christ. Let no man think he is without power or influence in this matter: let no man be apathetic, and listless or faint-hearted in his Redeemer's cause, and for His people's highest interests. Let each by prayer, by thought, speech, and behaviour do all that in him lies to turn the present occasion to its highest use. The mightiest aggregate of many million minds, which form the power of collective opinion and will, consists of individuals; and there is no individual who can declare himself free of that responsibility. It is the part of faith not only to *consider* such questions, but to proceed practically in working towards their *decision* according to the will of God. We are fettered by no iron fate. Let us be zealous for the Lord our God, to turn to His service and honour the course of this mortal life.

And here, brethren, I would point out one or two encouraging indications. In the first place, measuring from the year 1851, when eleven years ago there was a similar peaceful gathering of men from every nation in this capital, we have since been sorely chastened of the Lord; and whom the Lord *loveth* He chasteneth. The vain, delusive dreams of peace, philosophically grounded on mere worldly principles, which then filled many minds, soon were broken by a terrible awakening. The horrors of the Crimean war and the Indian mutiny have not been without their effect in teaching wisdom; and still more recent wars, and threaten-

ings of wars, together with the demonstration given
of the falsehood of those cobweb theories which
assumed that the world was to be governed by
mere market-price,—these things also have had
their effect. We are, I trust, as a nation more
sober-minded and less boastful than we were ten
years ago. Some of the more dangerous spirits are
moodily mourning over their fallen idol, and their
defeated expectations and predictions. The dollar
has not proved almighty, nor cotton king, nor
American institutions a safe specific and guarantee
of wisdom. And the straitened and suffering con-
dition of a great portion of our people has demon-
strated that there is folly and guilt in suffering the
bread of millions to depend for supplies on the
caprice of a single foreign market, out of the con-
temptuous disregard of every principle of wisdom
and prudence except the hand-to-mouth consideration of buying in the cheapest and selling in the
dearest. The chastening of the Lord has been laid
upon us, brethren: and truly we had need of it;
for never since the world began was there such a
race or such ardour for the worship of Mammon.
But the fruits of the chastisement may yet result in
blessing, if the Lord awaken us to His holy fear
and love by His gracious Spirit co-operating with
this discipline of His providence.

He has smitten us also near the throne, and by
the solemnity of that admonition has tempered our
too fervent pursuit of earthly things, and given a

higher aim to our reflections and aspirations. Doubtless it is good for us that we have been afflicted, if our souls be rightly exercised thereby; and though these bitter chastisements have wrought in us much sorrow, yet, happy for us, if they work in us some peaceable fruit of righteousness, if our sorrow have been after a godly sort, if our thoughts of the departed call our minds less exclusively to the scientific pursuit of the good things of this mortal life, and bid them ascend to fellowship with the holy and the blessed who are with Christ.

If, from the world of spirits, a soul that late had taken the liveliest and most influential interest in the arrangements for that great international gathering which is now begun, could return and speak his thoughts and views of these things now, what would be the lesson he would wish to impress most earnestly? Would it not be to set less on the mere perishable objects of this earth, and more upon rendering all things subservient to the kingdom and glory of the Redeemer, more upon the saving of the soul, and the building of the fabric of imperishable love?—more upon that motto which, on the suggestion of him 'for whom the nation has recently been mourning, was placed on the front of our civic Exchange, and remains there as a memorial and testimony to future ages, "THE EARTH IS THE LORD'S, AND THE FULNESS THEREOF?"

And I rejoice, brethren, that this occasion has been marked by a very express acknowledgment of Christ and of His sovereignty over all. The opening ceremonial of prayer and praise has given it a savour of His coming kingdom. The tones of its music were such as we know are heard and responded to in heaven, "HALLELUJAH! FOR THE LORD GOD OMNIPOTENT REIGNETH!" O may it please the Lord that on this occasion of the assembling of so many from every kindred, and people, and nation, and tongue, some Pentecostal outpouring of His Holy Spirit may be vouchsafed, and the season may be blessed to the turning of many hearts to the Lord, and the opening of many eyes to behold the light of His holy Word in plainer and clearer characters of faith and love!

The Lord grant to us that, so far as may depend on each of us, we may by word, by example, and in the unaffected feelings of our heart, by purity, by meekness, by piety and love, show forth the praises of Him who hath called us out of darkness into His marvellous light, and may draw others to the enjoyment of the same gracious privileges. We know not what change of scene may be in the near future, or how soon we may be summoned from this peaceful festival, even as happened after the last occasion, to the struggle and the conflict of war; but come what may of trial or of sorrow, let us with thankful hearts so improve this happy interlude of peace, that it may be to us as a time of refreshing from the presence of the Lord, and that we may proceed thenceforth with greater alacrity in His service, whether it be appointed us to act or to suffer for His name.

THE END.

GILBERT AND RIVINGTON, PRINTERS, ST. JOHN'S SQUARE, LONDON.